Learning Cursive Handwriting is
All About Practice

- ✓ Use your favourite pen or pencil.
- ✓ Find your comfortable posture (sitting position) and the right angle of your pen or pencil and the suitable position of your practice paper.
- ✓ Trace over the dotted letters repeatedly on the following pages, then start writing the letters on your own.
- ✓ Once Started, consider not to stop practicing until you get it right.
- ✓ It does not matter how it looks. Concentrate on the right form of the letter to make sure it is easy to read.

The more you practice, the better you get.
So, Keep Practicing...

This

Cursive Handwriting

Workbook belongs to

_____

- -

_____

_____

- -

_____

Uppercase Cursive Letters

A a B b C c D d

E e F f G g H h

I i J j K k L l

M m N n O o P p

Q q R r S s T t

U u V v W w X x

Y y Z z

Lowercase Cursive Letters

a a b b c c d d

e e f f g g h h

i i j j k k l l

m m n n o o p p

q q r r s s t t

u u v v w w x x

y y z z

a

a a a a a a a a a a a a a a a

a a a a a a a a a a a a a a a

a

a

a

a a a a a a a a a a a a a a a a a a a a

a a a a a a a a a a a a a a a a a a a a

a

a

B

BBBBBBBBBBBBBBBB

BBBBBBBBBBBBBBBB

B

B

b

b b b b b b b b b b b b b b b b b b b b b

b b b b b b b b b b b b b b b b b b b b b

b

b

C

C C C C C C C C C C C C C C C C C C C C

C C C C C C C C C C C C C C C C C C C

C

C

C

C C C C C C C C C C C C C C C C C C C C C C C C C C C C

C C C C C C C C C C C C C C C C C C C C C C C C C C C C

C

C

D

$\mathcal{D}$ $\mathcal{D}$ $\mathcal{D}$ $\mathcal{D}$ $\mathcal{D}$ $\mathcal{D}$ $\mathcal{D}$ $\mathcal{D}$ $\mathcal{D}$ $\mathcal{D}$ $\mathcal{D}$ $\mathcal{D}$ $\mathcal{D}$ $\mathcal{D}$ $\mathcal{D}$

$\mathcal{D}$ $\mathcal{D}$ $\mathcal{D}$ $\mathcal{D}$ $\mathcal{D}$ $\mathcal{D}$ $\mathcal{D}$ $\mathcal{D}$ $\mathcal{D}$ $\mathcal{D}$ $\mathcal{D}$ $\mathcal{D}$ $\mathcal{D}$ $\mathcal{D}$

$\mathcal{D}$

$\mathcal{D}$

d

d d d d d d d d d d d d d d d d d d d d d d d

d d d d d d d d d d d d d d d d d d d d d d d

d

d

Ɛ

Ɛ Ɛ

Ɛ Ɛ

Ɛ

Ɛ

e

e e e e e e e e e e e e e e e e e e e e e e e

e e e e e e e e e e e e e e e e e e e e e e e

e

e

F

F F F F F F F F F F F F F F F F F F F F F F F

F F F F F F F F F F F F F F F F F F F F

F

F

f

g

g g g g g g g g g g g g g g g g g g g g g g g g

g g g g g g g g g g g g g g g g g g g g g g g

g

g

H

H H H H H H H H H H H H H H H H

H H H H H H H H H H H H H H H H

H

H

h

h h h h h h h h h h h h h h h h h h h

h h h h h h h h h h h h h h h h h h h

h

h

l

l l l l l l l l l l l l l l l l l l l

l l l l l l l l l l l l l l l l l l l

l

l

i

i i i i i i i i i i i i i i i i i i i i i i i i i i i

i i i i i i i i i i i i i i i i i i i i i i i i i i i

i

i

$\mathcal{J}$

$\mathcal{J}$ $\mathcal{J}$ $\mathcal{J}$ $\mathcal{J}$ $\mathcal{J}$ $\mathcal{J}$ $\mathcal{J}$ $\mathcal{J}$ $\mathcal{J}$ $\mathcal{J}$ $\mathcal{J}$ $\mathcal{J}$ $\mathcal{J}$ $\mathcal{J}$ $\mathcal{J}$ $\mathcal{J}$ $\mathcal{J}$ $\mathcal{J}$ $\mathcal{J}$

$\mathcal{J}$ $\mathcal{J}$ $\mathcal{J}$ $\mathcal{J}$ $\mathcal{J}$ $\mathcal{J}$ $\mathcal{J}$ $\mathcal{J}$ $\mathcal{J}$ $\mathcal{J}$ $\mathcal{J}$ $\mathcal{J}$ $\mathcal{J}$ $\mathcal{J}$ $\mathcal{J}$ $\mathcal{J}$

$\mathcal{J}$

$\mathcal{J}$

j

jjjjjjjjjjjjjjjjjjjjjjjjjjjjjj

K

K K K K K K K K K K K K K K K K

K K K K K K K K K K K K K K K K

K

K

k

k k k k k k k k k k k k k k k k k k k k k k k

k k k k k k k k k k k k k k k k k k k k k k k k

k

k

$\mathcal{L}$

$\mathcal{L}$ $\mathcal{L}$ $\mathcal{L}$ $\mathcal{L}$ $\mathcal{L}$ $\mathcal{L}$ $\mathcal{L}$ $\mathcal{L}$ $\mathcal{L}$ $\mathcal{L}$ $\mathcal{L}$ $\mathcal{L}$ $\mathcal{L}$ $\mathcal{L}$ $\mathcal{L}$ $\mathcal{L}$ $\mathcal{L}$

$\mathcal{L}$ $\mathcal{L}$ $\mathcal{L}$ $\mathcal{L}$ $\mathcal{L}$ $\mathcal{L}$ $\mathcal{L}$ $\mathcal{L}$ $\mathcal{L}$ $\mathcal{L}$ $\mathcal{L}$ $\mathcal{L}$ $\mathcal{L}$ $\mathcal{L}$ $\mathcal{L}$ $\mathcal{L}$

$\mathcal{L}$

$\mathcal{L}$

ℓ

ℓℓℓℓℓℓℓℓℓℓℓℓℓℓℓℓℓℓℓℓℓℓℓℓℓℓ

ℓℓℓℓℓℓℓℓℓℓℓℓℓℓℓℓℓℓℓℓℓℓℓℓℓ

ℓ

ℓ

M

m m m m m m m m m m m m m m

m m m m m m m m m m m m m m

m

m

m

m m m m m m m m m m m m m m m

m m m m m m m m m m m m m m m

m

m

$\mathcal{N}$

$\mathcal{n}\ \mathcal{n}\ \mathcal{n}\ \mathcal{n}\ \mathcal{n}\ \mathcal{n}\ \mathcal{n}\ \mathcal{n}\ \mathcal{n}\ \mathcal{n}\ \mathcal{n}\ \mathcal{n}\ \mathcal{n}\ \mathcal{n}\ \mathcal{n}\ \mathcal{n}\ \mathcal{n}\ \mathcal{n}\ \mathcal{n}$

$\mathcal{n}\ \mathcal{n}\ \mathcal{n}\ \mathcal{n}\ \mathcal{n}\ \mathcal{n}\ \mathcal{n}\ \mathcal{n}\ \mathcal{n}\ \mathcal{n}\ \mathcal{n}\ \mathcal{n}\ \mathcal{n}\ \mathcal{n}\ \mathcal{n}\ \mathcal{n}\ \mathcal{n}$

$\mathcal{n}$

$\mathcal{n}$

n

n n n n n n n n n n n n n n n n n n n n n

m m m m m m m m m m m m m m m m m m m m m

m

m

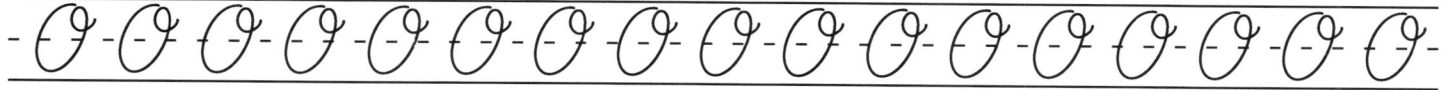

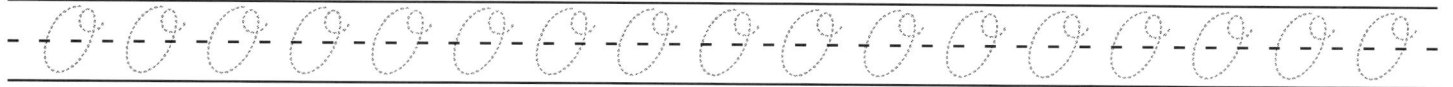

O

O O O O O O O O O O O O O O O O O O O O O O O O O O O O O O O

O O O O O O O O O O O O O O O O O O O O O O O O O O O O O O O

O

O

p

p p p p p p p p p p p p p p p p p p p p p

p p p p p p p p p p p p p p p p p p p p p

p

p

p

p p p p p p p p p p p p p p p p p p p p

p p p p p p p p p p p p p p p p p p p p

p

p

Q

QQQQQQQQQQQQQQQQQQQQQQ

QQQQQQQQQQQQQQQQQQQQ

Q

Q

q

q q q q q q q q q q q q q q q q q q q q q q q q q q

q q q q q q q q q q q q q q q q q q q q q q q q q

q

q

R

RRRRRRRRRRRRRRRRRR

RRRRRRRRRRRRRRRRR

R

R

n

n n n n n n n n n n n n n n n n n n n n n n n n n n n n

n n n n n n n n n n n n n n n n n n n n n n n n n n n

n

n

$\mathcal{S}$

$\mathcal{S}$ $\mathcal{S}$ $\mathcal{S}$ $\mathcal{S}$ $\mathcal{S}$ $\mathcal{S}$ $\mathcal{S}$ $\mathcal{S}$ $\mathcal{S}$ $\mathcal{S}$ $\mathcal{S}$ $\mathcal{S}$ $\mathcal{S}$ $\mathcal{S}$ $\mathcal{S}$ $\mathcal{S}$ $\mathcal{S}$

$\mathcal{S}$

$\mathcal{S}\,\mathcal{S}$

T

$\mathcal{T}$ $\mathcal{T}$ $\mathcal{T}$ $\mathcal{T}$ $\mathcal{T}$ $\mathcal{T}$ $\mathcal{T}$ $\mathcal{T}$ $\mathcal{T}$ $\mathcal{T}$ $\mathcal{T}$ $\mathcal{T}$ $\mathcal{T}$ $\mathcal{T}$ $\mathcal{T}$ $\mathcal{T}$

$\mathcal{T}$ $\mathcal{T}$ $\mathcal{T}$ $\mathcal{T}$ $\mathcal{T}$ $\mathcal{T}$ $\mathcal{T}$ $\mathcal{T}$ $\mathcal{T}$ $\mathcal{T}$ $\mathcal{T}$ $\mathcal{T}$ $\mathcal{T}$ $\mathcal{T}$ $\mathcal{T}$

$\mathcal{T}$

$\mathcal{T}$

t

t t t t t t t t t t t t t t t t t t t t t t t t t

t t t t t t t t t t t t t t t t t t t t t t t t t

t

t

U

U U U U U U U U U U U U U U U U U U

U U U U U U U U U U U U U U U U U U

U

U

$\mathcal{U}$

$\mathcal{U}$ $\mathcal{U}$ $\mathcal{U}$ $\mathcal{U}$ $\mathcal{U}$ $\mathcal{U}$ $\mathcal{U}$ $\mathcal{U}$ $\mathcal{U}$ $\mathcal{U}$ $\mathcal{U}$ $\mathcal{U}$ $\mathcal{U}$ $\mathcal{U}$ $\mathcal{U}$ $\mathcal{U}$ $\mathcal{U}$ $\mathcal{U}$ $\mathcal{U}$ $\mathcal{U}$

$\mathcal{V}$

$\mathcal{V}$ $\mathcal{V}$ $\mathcal{V}$ $\mathcal{V}$ $\mathcal{V}$ $\mathcal{V}$ $\mathcal{V}$ $\mathcal{V}$ $\mathcal{V}$ $\mathcal{V}$ $\mathcal{V}$ $\mathcal{V}$ $\mathcal{V}$ $\mathcal{V}$ $\mathcal{V}$ $\mathcal{V}$ $\mathcal{V}$ $\mathcal{V}$

v v v v v v v v v v v v v v v v v v v

v

v

n

W

𝒲 𝒲 𝒲 𝒲 𝒲 𝒲 𝒲 𝒲 𝒲 𝒲 𝒲 𝒲 𝒲 𝒲 𝒲 𝒲

𝒲 𝒲 𝒲 𝒲 𝒲 𝒲 𝒲 𝒲 𝒲 𝒲 𝒲 𝒲 𝒲 𝒲 𝒲 𝒲

𝒲

𝒲

W

W W W W W W W W W W W W W W W W W W

X

X X X X X X X X X X X X X X X X X X

X X X X X X X X X X X X X X X X X X

X

X

x

x x x x x x x x x x x x x x x x x x x x x

Y

Y Y Y Y Y Y Y Y Y Y Y Y Y Y Y Y Y Y Y Y

Y Y Y Y Y Y Y Y Y Y Y Y Y Y Y Y Y Y Y Y

Y

Y

Y

Y Y Y Y Y Y Y Y Y Y Y Y Y Y Y Y Y

Y Y Y Y Y Y Y Y Y Y Y Y Y Y Y Y Y

Y

Y

Z

Z Z Z Z Z Z Z Z Z Z Z Z Z Z Z Z Z

Z Z Z Z Z Z Z Z Z Z Z Z Z Z Z Z

Z

Z

Z

Z Z Z Z Z Z Z Z Z Z Z Z Z Z Z Z Z Z Z Z

Z Z Z Z Z Z Z Z Z Z Z Z Z Z Z Z Z Z Z Z

First, let's practice writing a few sentences.

Apples taste good.

Apples taste good.

Apples are tasty.

Apples are tasty.

Now, let's practice writing a few sentences.

Boys like to play.

Boys like to play.

Boys love toys.

Boys love toys.

Try practice writing these sentences.

Cats meow.

Cats meow.

Cats purr.

Cats purr.

Now, let's practice writing these sentences.

Dogs bark.

Dogs bark.

Dogs dig.

Dogs dig.

First, let's practice writing a few sentences.

Eggs taste good.

Eggs taste good.

Eggs break.

Eggs break.

Now, let's practice writing these sentences.

Football is fun.

Football is fun.

Fly a kite.

Fly a kite.

Let's practice writing these sentences.

Go outside.

Go outside.

Giggle with me.

Giggle with me.

Try practice writing these sentences.

Hello friend.

Hello friend.

High in the sky.

High in the sky.

First, let's practice writing a few sentences.

Ice is cold.

Ice is cold.

Igloos are cool.

Igloos are cool.

Let's practice writing these sentences.

Jelly is good.

Jelly is good.

Jam is better.

Jam is better.

Now let's practice writing these sentences.

Kings rule.

Kings rule.

Keys open doors.

Keys open doors.

Try practice writing these sentences.

Leaves on trees.

Leaves on trees.

Lamps are bright.

Lamps are bright.

Let's practice writing these sentences.

Mice love cheese.

Mice love cheese.

Monsters are scary.

Monsters are scary.

Next, let's write these sentences.

Noses itch.

Noses itch.

Nicely done.

Nicely done.

Try practice writing these sentences.

Owls fly.

Owls fly.

Owls are birds.

Owls are birds.

Next, let's write these sentences.

Pandas are cute.

Pandas are cute.

Puppies are playful.

Puppies are playful.

Try writing these sentences next.

Questions are good.

Questions are good.

Quails are birds.

Quails are birds.

Try practice writing these sentences.

Roses smell good.

Roses smell good.

Red is pretty.

Red is pretty.

First, let's practice writing a few sentences.

School is cool.

School is cool.

Sun shines bright.

Sun shines bright.

Try writing these sentences next.

Toys are fun.

Toys are fun.

Tiny is cute.

Tiny is cute.

Now, let's practice writing these sentences.

Up there.

Up there.

Up and down.

Up and down.

Try practice writing these sentences.

Vans are cool.

Vans are cool.

Violas sound nice.

Violas sound nice.

First, let's practice writing a few sentences.

Watch me write.

Watch me write.

Write right.

Write right.

First, let's practice writing a few sentences.

Xenon is a gas.

Xenon is a gas.

X-rays work.

X-rays work.

First, let's practice writing a few sentences.

Yams are tasty.

Yams are tasty.

Yummy food.

Yummy food.

First, let's practice writing a few sentences.

Zip zap zit.

Zip zap zit.

Zoom or boom.

Zoom or boom.

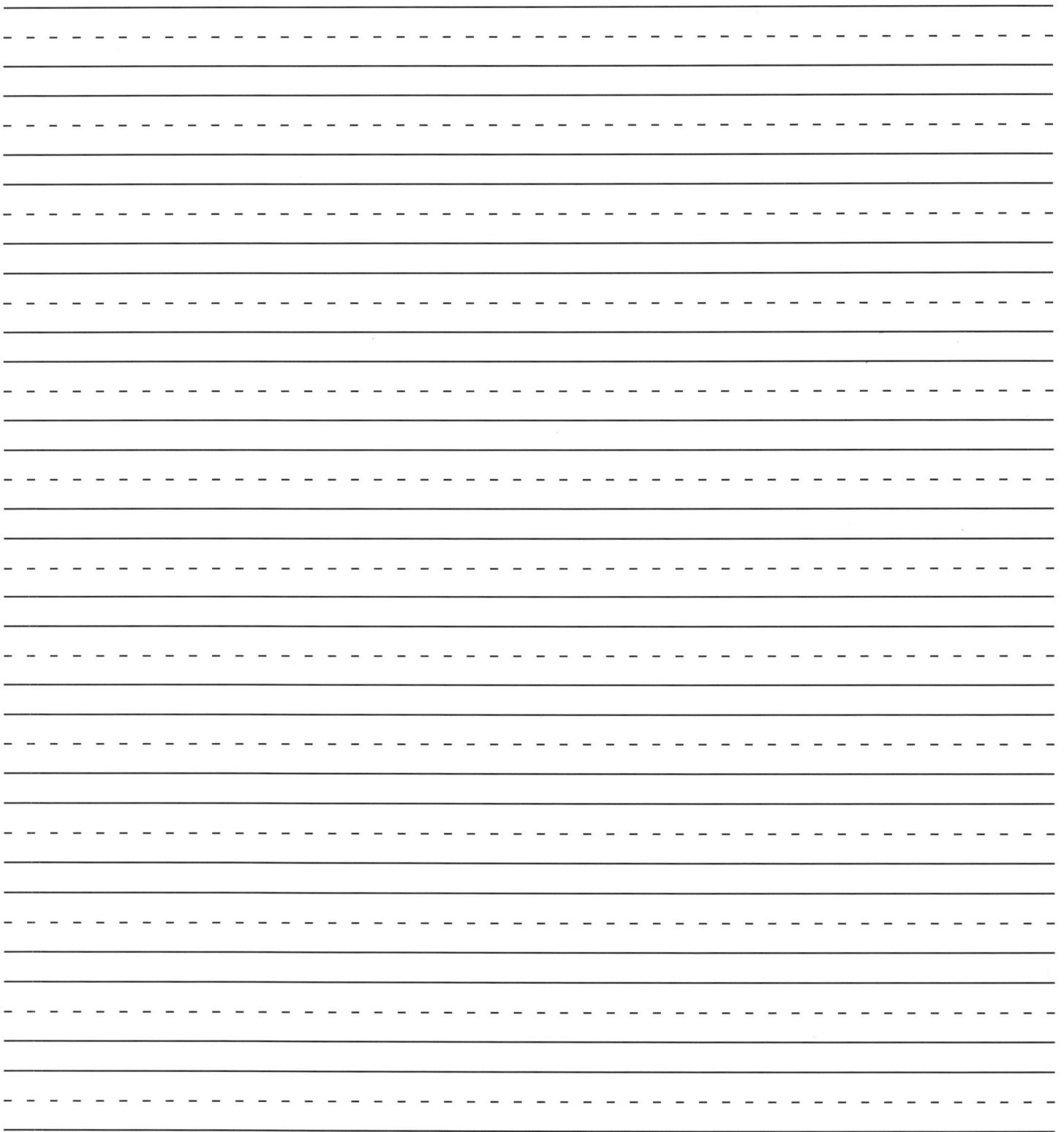